BERWICK BAR
AND FORTIFIC...

NORTHUMBERLAND

Doreen Grove

Inspector of Ancient Monuments, Historic Scotland

The bustling town of Berwick sits on the north bank of the River Tweed, at the east end of the long-disputed border between Scotland and England. Given its strategic position, it is perhaps not surprising that it became one of the outstanding fortified towns of Europe. Control of Berwick passed back and forth between Scotland and England until 1482. Each successive crisis brought repairs and improvements to the fortifications. But it is the defences, built from 1558, that best illustrate the scale of resources invested in Berwick – an investment that continued long after the border had ceased to be an issue. Soldiers were billeted on the townspeople until the early eighteenth century, when barracks were constructed.

This guidebook provides a tour of the buildings and fortifications associated with Berwick-upon-Tweed's military past, and gives an account of the construction of the walls and barracks. It also provides an insight into the lives of the soldiers who spent many weary hours patrolling the walls.

❖ CONTENTS ❖

Published by English Heritage 23 Savile Row, London W1S 2ET
© English Heritage 1999 First published by English Heritage 1999,
reprinted 2002
Photographs by English Heritage Photographic Unit and copyright
of English Heritage, unless otherwise stated.

Edited by Susannah Lawson. Designed by Pauline Hull. Plans by Hardlines
Printed in England by Sterling Press
C30 03/02 04754 ISBN 1 85074 728 8

INTRODUCTION

'...*the English possess beyond the eastern arm of the sea, named Tivida [the Tweed] in the kingdom of Scotland, the singular fortress of Berwick... which is a very strong place both by nature and art...*'

(C. A. Sneyd (ed.), *A Relation of the Island of England about the Year 1500*, Camden Society, no. 37, 1847, p.17)

The fortifications of Berwick-upon-Tweed are among the finest in Britain. The thirteenth-century town walls had to withstand an army equipped with scaling ladders and medieval siege artillery. They were adapted and eventually redesigned over the next 400 years, as military engineers struggled to take account of guns. Berwick served as a testing-ground for the development of the architecture and weaponry of warfare. But when change came, it was often slow, always under-funded and invariably prompted by a crisis.

The numerous soldiers inflicted on the town throughout medieval times were often bored and frequently poor. The government was no better at paying soldiers regularly than it was at maintaining the walls. The effect on people living here was profound. The impact of a regular garrison in a small town was significant enough, but the billeting of many thousands of men in times of crisis must have been unbearable. Townspeople were forever complaining that 'the Quartering and Billeting of Soldiers in Garrison here is very troublesome and inconvenient to the people'. The complaints continued until the barracks were completed in 1721.

Berwick from the north-east, with the barracks in the foreground

TOUR OF THE BARRACKS

❖

The gateway to the barracks

The emblazoned arms of George I over the gateway

The tour starts in the barrack square, just outside the shop, at the information panel which shows a plan of the barracks.

'King George since his Accession to the Throne, to ease the Inhabitants of this town from quartering of Soldiers, hath built a fine Barrack here.'
(John Macky, *A Journey through England and Scotland,* 1724)

As you entered the shop and ticket office, you will have walked through the main entrance to Berwick Barracks beneath a round-topped gateway, decorated with the arms of George I. On one side of the gatehouse was the 'black hole', or prison, which was later rebuilt as the officers' mess, and on the other side was the guardhouse (now the shop). Even today, it is easy to imagine the shouted commands of a sergeant major in the square.

In 1717, the Board of Ordnance, the government department responsible for the construction and maintenance of fortifications, ordered the construction of barracks in Berwick. They were designed to house 600 men and 36 officers and were expected to cost £4,937-10s-6d. Mr Macky, a visitor in 1724, thought that the very concept of purpose-built barracks was remarkable. 'These are the first Barracks erected in Great Britain: and it would be a vast Ease to the Inhabitants in most great Towns if they had them every where, but English Liberty will never consent to what will seem a Nest for a Standing Army.' Although mistaken about them being the first, he sums up the novelty of the barracks and the mistrust of the army felt by most of the population in the eighteenth century.

Berwick has two three-storey blocks of

barracks facing each other across the square. A stores building, known as the Clock Block, on the south side (directly opposite) completes the square. The west barrack (on the right) remains in military use and is not open to visitors.

There are several reasons why barracks were constructed here at Berwick in the eighteenth century. The number of soldiers in the town had changed little over the centuries and the town authorities had campaigned ceaselessly for relief. Since Berwick had no fitting soldiers' lodgings, like those found in royal castles such as Tynemouth or Edinburgh, soldiers were billeted in alehouses. This was good neither for military discipline, nor for order in the town. The option for change first arose in 1705, and four years later, in the following appeal to their Member of Parliament, the town authorities explained the problem and proposed this new solution:

The case of the alehouse keepers in town being represented to this Guild to be very lamentable with respect to their quartereing ye Soldiers sent here above what they are able insomuch that severall persons that Formerly sold Ale on which their lively hood Chiefly depended have been Obleiged to Leave of the Trade by which those that still Use it are daily more burdened; It is therefore hereby Ordered that ye Case be prepaired by Mr Mayor and sent to our Members of Parliement to be presented to her Majestie [Queen Anne] by them that an Order may be got for the building of barracks without which those poor people Can never be eased Solong as Soldiers are Continued here.

(*Berwick Guild Book,* Records Office, Berwick-upon-Tweed, 28 October 1709)

The barrack square

The barracks seen from the Elizabethan walls. The gymnasium is on the right

Their appeals fell on deaf ears until 1715, when the Jacobite Rising shook the Government out of its complacency. Berwick was acknowledged as a useful staging-post between Scotland and England, and in March 1716, 'Parliament granted the charges of erecting barracks in this garrison'.

The origin of the design of the barracks remains something of a mystery. Nicholas Hawksmoor, one of the finest architects of his day, was almost certainly responsible. Yet no trace survives of his appointment by the Board of Ordnance or of him having visited Berwick. The earliest drawing, dated 20 May 1717, although unsigned, is almost certainly in his hand. But there his involvement probably ended, as there are major differences between the initial drawing and the final building. The board's engineer, Captain Thomas

Phillips, took the basic design and altered it to fit the particular circumstances he faced in Berwick. Lost are the elegantly curved gable ends to the barracks, and the façades have been greatly simplified. Problems with the gateway caused another Board of Ordnance builder, Andrews Jelfe, to be summoned to alter Hawksmoor's original design.

A major refit in 1799 altered the barracks considerably. The characteristic raised sections of cornice, that gave the impression of eyebrows, were removed. Although this was not what Hawksmoor had intended, they did relieve the long, forbidding frontage of the barracks (see illustration on page 25). All of the floors and windows were replaced and, on the ground and second floors, the round-headed window surrounds were replaced with square ones. The new

The earliest known drawing of the barracks, dated 1717. Although unsigned, it is almost certainly by Nicholas Hawksmoor

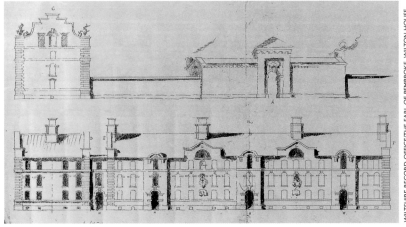

cookhouse, built behind the barracks, would be of 'great convenience, as formerly each soldier had to prepare his victuals in his own room'. It continued to be used right up to the present century. Latrine blocks attached to the barracks in the nineteenth century replaced a wash house that originally stood in the barrack square. These too were later removed.

Walk across the square and go through door 'B' on the left.

The Soldiers' Barracks

This was once the soldiers' barracks. The block now houses an exhibition about army life, called 'By Beat of Drum'. It includes a reconstruction of an eighteenth-century barrack room and a nineteenth-century regimental schoolroom.

At Berwick there are 72 barrack rooms, almost all identical, which are reached from six sets of stairs (three in each block). Each staircase has three landings with four rooms leading off. Each room had a window and a fireplace, and was designed to take four double beds, sleeping eight men. A table and benches stood in the centre of the room, along with a slop bucket, which had to be emptied every morning.

These small rooms were home to their occupants. The men cooked their rations over the fire and ate them at the same table at which they

---

❖ A SOLDIER'S ❖ WAGE

A soldier's life may appear harsh by today's standards, but pay was regular (in theory, at least) and the army provided a bed of sorts, as well as food, clothing and security – conditions and comfort that poor agricultural workers might struggle to achieve. That said, when a young farm boy took 'the king's shilling' to enlist in the army, he did not find a life of luxury. Pay was twelve pence (five new pence) a day. Over and above the six pence docked for rations, soldiers like William Cobbett faced additional charges for 'washing, mending, soap, flour for hair-powder, shoes, stockings, shirts, stocks and gaiters, pipe-clay and several other things', leaving them with very little for themselves or their families.

---

cleaned their uniforms and weapons. The only large communal space was the barrack square, mainly because uncontrolled groups of soldiers could be a threat to order. Shortages of blankets, coal and food were common. Although there were rules governing the quantity of rations, the quality was variable and food was very often barely edible. An Edinburgh landlady once remarked that 'it taks a deal o' dirt to poison sogers'. It is very difficult to imagine what it must have been like for the soldiers to live in such a confined space, with a slop bucket and without bathing facilities. Despite these conditions, soldiers from

A volley of musket rounds reverberates around the barrack square during this recent re-enactment

Reconstructions of an eighteenth-century barrack room (above), and a nineteenth-century regimental schoolroom (above right) in the 'By Beat of Drum' exhibition at Berwick

Berwick fought successfully all over the Empire, and their achievements should not be forgotten. As Private Wheeler wrote in 1813, 'But who shall record the glorious deeds of the soldier whose lot is numbered with the thousands in the ranks who live and die and fight in obscurity.'

The Gymnasium

After you have finished walking round the barrack rooms, follow the path round to the rear of the block to the gymnasium.

This building now houses a contemporary art gallery, showing a wide range of temporary exhibitions. A gymnasium is very much a feature of the modern army – an organisation that recognises the importance of physical training for an efficient fighting force. Improvements came along with public interest in the morals and well-being of the soldiers, resulting in reforms to all aspects of army life. Corruption among officers

was tackled, physical punishments, such as flogging, were abolished and great efforts were made to educate soldiers. Libraries were encouraged, savings schemes introduced and pastimes devised to keep men away from beer and spirits. Sports and games became increasingly important as part of army life.

The Clock Block

Return to the barrack square and turn left into the Clock Block.

This now houses the Borough Museum and Art Gallery, which includes an exhibition on the history of Berwick, and a collection of paintings and ceramics donated to the town by Sir William Burrell, the Glasgow shipping magnate and a great collector of art.

The Clock Block was built soon after 1739 to replace an earlier powder magazine on the site. It might have been designed as part of the original barracks, although it does not feature in the surviving 1717 drawings. In spite of this, the design betrays many of the details that Nicholas Hawksmoor used elsewhere, and it is possible that he produced it, but that construction only followed when funds became available.

This grand, three-storey store house has a central staircase leading to six large rooms. It was used to store everything from 'drawers, woollen, long' to bully-beef (tinned meat) and knapsacks, and remained in use until

1964, by which time the ground floor had acquired the additional role of kitchen and dining-room.

When you have finished looking round the Clock Block, go back out into the square and enter door 'O'.

The Officers' Barracks

This block was once the officers' barracks. It now serves as the regimental headquarters and museum of the King's Own Scottish Borderers.

Raised in Edinburgh in 1689 as Leven's Regiment, the King's Own Scottish Borderers have a long and gallant history, serving in most of the major wars since that time. Berwick was their depot from 1881 until 1964, when they marched out of the barracks for the last time. Strong links are maintained through their splendid regimental museum, which includes uniforms, medals, old army rations and medical supplies, as well as a reconstruction of the officers' mess

BOTH PICTURES: BOROUGH MUSEUM AND ART GALLERY

The River Touques *by Eugene Boudin, 1891 and* Russian Dancers *by Edgar Degas, c.1900, two paintings from the Borough Museum and Art Gallery, housed in the Clock Block*

❖ THE EVILS OF DRINK ❖

NATIONAL ARMY MUSEUM, LONDON

Drink and boredom were the enemies of good order in the army, and many men were drawn into a culture of excess. It was not until the nineteenth century that any attempt was made to encourage good behaviour by providing married quarters, schooling, libraries and fitness regimes. 'Picture if you can a...room with...beds 18 inches apart and in the centre the table with plates and basins upon them and perhaps the bread and butter for the next day's consumption.

The Corporal in Good Quarters, *after Thomas Rowlandson, 1812*

On and in the beds are the men, some... lying full-dressed on the beds in a semi-drunken stupor occasionally muttering curses, others smoking and some snoring, try and picture this and you will have some slight idea of the misery endured by a steady young man in the army in hundreds of barrack rooms in the country.' A sorry image provided by one of the new breed of soldiers in the mid-nineteenth century who saw the army as a profession and not just a job.

room. Unlike the soldiers' barracks, the officers' accommodation is more spacious, with a light and airy corridor running north to south through the block. The privilege of rank is clear from the size and number of the rooms: there are 24 rooms for 36 officers. Each of the senior officers had his own room, while the junior officers shared, two to a room, until 1799, when additional rooms were provided in the town and only duty officers remained in the barracks.

This completes your tour of the barracks. Return to the entrance and retrace your steps through the shop. If you would like to begin the tour of the fortifications, turn right and go through the gate on to the ramparts at the end of the barracks.

Top left, centre and bottom left: Photographs taken for a regimental recruiting brochure in 1939. Top right: The depot in 1955. Bottom right: Final departure of the King's Own Scottish Borderers in November 1963

TOUR OF THE FORTIFICATIONS

The bird's-eye view of the fortifications on page 18 and the town plan on the inside back cover will help you to follow the route and to find the sections of wall visible above ground. The tour starts at Windmill Bastion and goes round the walls clockwise, taking detours to see the Main Guard, the Governor's House and the hospital. The tour of the walls is a rewarding two miles, but it can be divided into convenient lengths (the town has excellent cafés and tea shops). For a short visit, the length from Windmill Bastion to King's Mount (see below) gives a good impression of the Elizabethan walls, with medieval work visible beyond. The principles of fortifications are explained under the section on Windmill Bastion.

Windmill Bastion

Turn right along the ramparts with the barracks and gymnasium on your right, then climb to the top of the bastion on your left.

The tour of the fortifications starts at Windmill Bastion because it is an excellent vantage point with panoramic views. Its position ensured the strategic importance of this area of the defences and the successive attempts to defend the town remain visible here.

Aerial view of Windmill Bastion looking south

Windmill Bastion is the larger of the two complete, regular bastions on the Elizabethan walls. Work on it began between 1563 and 1564 and was completed, except for the cavalier, by 1570 (that took a further 70 years and another crisis to complete). The construction of the Elizabethan walls followed a standard plan. The five bastions are gun-platforms protruding from the wall at the points where it changes direction, or at the centre of long, straight stretches. Each had guns which were carefully aligned so as to protect the wall and ditch and the face of the next bastion with the smallest possible number of guns and

men. Crossfire from these guns left no vulnerable blind spots and this forms the basic principal behind this type of fortification. Gun-chambers called 'flankers' lay at the rear of the angle-pointed bastions, where their guns could scour the ditch. The massive earth platform, or 'cavalier' on top of each bastion held heavy field guns to cover the approach and a lower earth parapet protected smaller guns covering the ditch and counterscarp (see diagram below). Criticised during construction for being too narrow and inconvenient, the flankers were altered. The idea of an upper gun-deck was abandoned, and the side walls were cut back, widened and refaced and the front wall of the flankers rebuilt. (These changes are most obvious at Cumberland Bastion.)

The clear field of fire for the guns was provided by an area of ground sloping away beyond the ditch called the 'glacis'. At its inner edge a 'covert' or covered way provided a safe path for defending soldiers leaving the ditch and patrolling the outworks. The ditch originally held water and had a wall or 'counterscarp' on the outer edge and a flat base running up to the main face of the wall. A stone outer wall, or 'scarp', held the ramparts and bastions, that formed the main defence, in place. This scarp slopes gently inwards to a half-round cordon, designed to throw off a cannon ball running up

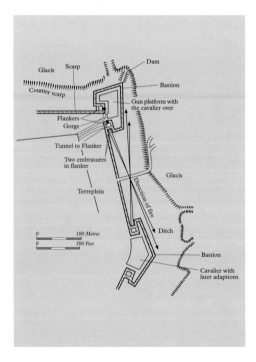

Diagram to show the angles of fire from Windmill to Brass Bastion

the face of the wall. Behind the stone parapet a sentry path was planned and beyond this, an earth parapet 16 feet high. Sentries used the top of the ramparts, known as the 'terreplein', as a fighting platform and a walkway. The stone parapet was at the same height as the counterscarp of the ditch, so that a shot fired from the far side of the ditch would sink into the mounded earth parapet above the scarp.

The medieval wall that protected the town from the thirteenth to the sixteenth century was once 50 feet high and 12 feet wide. It is now reduced to a low, earth-covered mound, and a section of it lies just to the east of this bastion (straight ahead of you). Beyond it is the D-shaped ditched earthwork known as the Bulwark in the Snook, built between 1522 and 1523. Just to the south can be seen the faint traces of Edward VI's citadel, designed in 1550 to provide a secure alternative to Berwick Castle – a bolthole should the town be captured.

Unlike the remainder of the walls, Windmill Bastion continued to be used until the present century. After 1859 it was adapted as a coastal defence battery during a major rearming of the British coastline. Alterations made to the earthworks of the bastion to take modern guns, some with rails for manoeuvring guns, can still be seen on the two upper gun platforms. (The guns

were removed at the end of the First World War.) The final use came during the Second World War, when anti-aircraft guns replaced the 12-pounders, the ditch became a physical training ground and the north flanker served as a 25-yard rifle range.

Walk back down the path and turn left.

The Magazine

Between Windmill Bastion and King's Mount, on the right, is the magazine, where gunpowder was stored. It was designed and built between 1749 and 1750 by Dugall Campbell, an engineer working for the Board of Ordnance. (The building is not normally open to visitors.) The 624 barrels of gunpowder were protected by a vaulted and buttressed building, designed to send a blast upwards should the powder be accidentally

Top: magazine regulations on the door. Above: gunpowder barrels. Below: The powder Magazine with the Lions House in the distance

King's Mount, which never had an upper gun platform or cavalier

Fisher's Fort, with the blocked water gate at the south end

ignited. However, avoiding the possibility of such a disaster was a considerable part of the design. All metal in the building is non-ferrous, to avoid accidental sparks, the air vents are 'Y'-shaped to ensure stray sparks could not enter the building, and a special timber-lifting gantry was installed for moving the barrels inside. Special magazine clothes and soft boots had to be worn.

Carry on along the path until you reach King's Mount.

King's Mount

The line of the medieval walls is still visible beyond the ramparts between Windmill Bastion and King's Mount. King's Mount, like its sister bastion Meg's Mount, was only half built. The southern half of the bastion was built against the medieval walls, while a decision was made as to how best to complete the new circuit. The most defensive line would have run across town to join Meg's Mount.

Indeed, this line was chosen and work began, but stopped almost at once, because a significant part of the town would have been left unprotected.

Carry on along the path by the river.

The Riverside Walls to Coxon's Tower

The wall along the river from King's Mount to Coxon's Tower is essentially the medieval wall, although there are several considerable sections of eighteenth-century repair. There was once a series of semicircular towers that punctuated the walls at regular intervals. One of these is still standing – the Blackwatch Tower, which stands in a shallow bend of the walls very close to King's Mount.

Like all the others, it was reduced in height in the late fifteenth or early sixteenth century, when it was converted to a gun tower. In 1533 the main wall of the tower was described as '8 foot thick and...so riven and in such decay as the gunners dare not occupy any piece of ordnance with the same for doubt of falling thereof'. The remainder of this section of wall, as it descends past Ness Gate, was similarly condemned. It once contained two further towers, the Watchhouse Tower and Plumber's Tower, roughly at either end of what is now known as Fisher's Fort, one of the sections rebuilt in the eighteenth century. On top of it stands a Russian gun from the Crimean War. Beneath it, visible from the beach, is a blocked water gate. The wall from here to Coxon's Tower was entirely rebuilt in the eighteenth century.

Carry on along the path until you reach Coxon's Tower. Walk up the steps to the top of the tower.

Coxon's Tower and Palace Green

Coxon's Tower, originally known as the Bulwark in the Sands, is a quarter-round tower at the river's edge, constructed in 1491 to protect the walls from naval attack. It has a lower vaulted chamber (which you can see when you go back down the two flights of stairs) and an upper gun deck.

At the west end of the line of embrasures beyond the tower, a road leads right into Palace Green. At the end is the Main Guard.

Coxon's Tower and the quay walls from the south

The Main Guard stood in Marygate until it was moved to Palace Green in 1815

The Governor's House

Above: The medieval quayside wall. Right: The old bridge, seen from the south shore of the Tweed

The Main Guard and the Governor's House

The Main Guard is a guardhouse that used to stand in Marygate. In 1815 a proposal was made to build a new one near Scotsgate, but this was rejected in favour of this site. It is possible that the builders might have reused some of the materials from the earlier building but replaced the rustic arches with a more classical portico, so altering the frontage. Recently repaired for Berwick Civic Society by English Heritage, it now houses two informative exhibitions. On the far side of Palace Green is the Governor's House, built in 1719, and described at the end of the century by Dr Fuller as a 'pretty stone building, three stories [sic] in height'. It is, perhaps, another of Nicholas Hawksmoor's designs. (It is in private ownership and not open to visitors.)

Re-join the riverside walk by the Main Guard, turning to the right.

The Quay Walls

Much of the riverside wall up to Meg's Mount was rebuilt in the eighteenth century and part of the quay walls, just west of Coxon's Tower, was realigned. Houses began to encroach onto the back of the quay walls in the eighteenth century; one of the finest is the Customs House at number 18, built in 1800. The number of passages through to the shore from the town echoes this erosion of the security of the walls. These were in addition to the official breaches at Shoregate, a medieval gate rebuilt in the eighteenth century, and a sallyport near the bridge.

The old bridge has had a chequered history. A great storm in 1199 swept away the first recorded bridge. Its replacement was damaged in 1216 and rebuilt about 1285, only to be swept away a second time. Thereafter, the town survived for a long period without a bridge although it is clear from the construction of a Brighouse gate

'which opens out towards England' in 1313 that a replacement was intended. In the event, they probably waited until 1401. A further rebuilding was necessary in 1490 and in 1634 the present stone, multi-arched bridge finally replaced the earlier bridges. Altered in the eighteenth century, the gate was finally removed in 1825. Beyond the old bridge, the walls carry on up to Meg's Mount, beneath the Royal Tweed Road Bridge, built in 1928. The wall from the river to Meg's Mount rises in three steps. It was rebuilt for Charles I and then altered in the eighteenth century. It is possible to follow the walls around Meg's Mount and return to the town through Scotsgate. But the tour will take the riverside path and follow the medieval walls to the castle.

The Medieval Walls to the Castle

The path along the river runs towards the magnificent Royal Border Bridge, built between 1847 and 1850 by Robert Stephenson to carry the North British railway over the Tweed. The railway line runs right through the middle of the castle (it had already been robbed of much of its stone for buildings in the town). High on the steep overgrown riverbank, at least two short sections of medieval wall remain above ground, one close to Meg's Mount.

Just before the viaduct, turn right through the stone gates and up some steps.

At the top of this path is the only section of the east face of the castle now visible – a tower at the extreme south-east corner, known as the Constable's Tower. It is a particularly fine, fourteenth-century polygonal tower, with fishtail arrow-slits in the beautifully coursed masonry. (It stands in private ground, but is visible from the public footpath.)

Go back down the steps and return to the riverside path. Carry on along the path to the castle.

From here you can see the spectacular White Wall steps. Begun in 1296, the parapet is stepped and has loops for arrows. The wall-walk is, for obvious reasons, called Breakneck Stairs! Originally, the White Wall ran from the castle down into the river and by 1392, it terminated in a tower. This had been swept away by floods by around 1540 and replaced with a gun tower.

Constable's Tower, which formed the southern corner of Berwick Castle. The quality of the stonework provides a tantalising hint of the quality of buildings swept away

The White Wall and Breakneck Stairs from the gun emplacement on the riverbank

BERWICK-UPON-TWEED

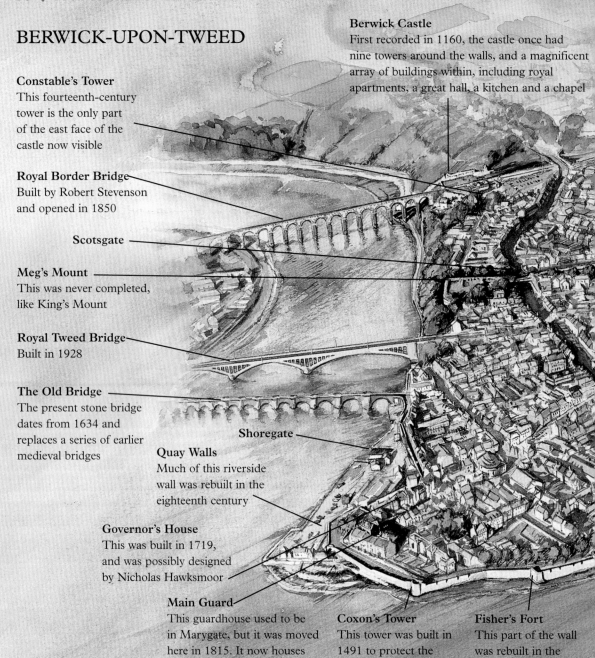

Berwick Castle
First recorded in 1160, the castle once had nine towers around the walls, and a magnificent array of buildings within, including royal apartments, a great hall, a kitchen and a chapel

Constable's Tower
This fourteenth-century tower is the only part of the east face of the castle now visible

Royal Border Bridge
Built by Robert Stevenson and opened in 1850

Scotsgate

Meg's Mount
This was never completed, like King's Mount

Royal Tweed Bridge
Built in 1928

The Old Bridge
The present stone bridge dates from 1634 and replaces a series of earlier medieval bridges

Shoregate

Quay Walls
Much of this riverside wall was rebuilt in the eighteenth century

Governor's House
This was built in 1719, and was possibly designed by Nicholas Hawksmoor

Main Guard
This guardhouse used to be in Marygate, but it was moved here in 1815. It now houses exhibitions

Coxon's Tower
This tower was built in 1491 to protect the walls from naval attack

Fisher's Fort
This part of the wall was rebuilt in the eighteenth century

Cumberland Bastion
This is one of the earliest and best preserved of the bastions. Like Windmill, it is a complete bastion

Bell Tower
Originally built in 1392, this bell tower was remodelled in 1577. The last bell was rung in 1683

Lord's Mount
This massive, curved stone bulwark was built in the 1540s to protect the walls at their weakest point

Brass Bastion
This is the point where the old and new walls meet. Brass Bastion was built between 1563 and 1564

The Hospital
69a Ravensdowne was built in 1745 as a military hospital

The Traverse
Built in 1564–5 to protect the vulnerable east flank of the town

Cowport
The only original gateway in the Elizabethan ramparts

Barracks
Built after the 1715 Jacobite Rising to provide permanent accommodation for soldiers

Windmill Bastion
Built between 1563 and 1570, this bastion enjoys an excellent vantage point, with panoramic views

Remains of Edward VI's Citadel
Designed in 1550, this provided a secure alternative to Berwick Castle

Magazine
This is where gunpowder was stored. The building was designed between 1749 and 1750

Ness Gate
Built in 1815

Blackwatch Tower
This is the best-preserved of the semicircular towers that punctuated the medieval walls at regular intervals

King's Mount
This bastion meets the medieval walls and was only ever half built

PETER DUNN

The west wall of the castle and the White Wall, seen from the Tweed

The ground floor of this postern tower has cramped casemates for three guns – uncomfortable by any standards, despite the provision of smoke vents. The upper gun-floor was once equipped with small swivel guns. The gunners here at least had the benefits of a fireplace, traces of which are still visible on your right (if you are standing just by the arch over the path). The tower probably had a further storey of guns behind embrasure parapets. The path continues through the vaulted passage in the tower.

Go along the riverside path and take the steep track up to the right.

The west wall of the castle survives because it served as the railway yard wall. A second gun-tower can be seen protruding from the castle. Built

in the sixteenth century, it provided cover for the west face of the castle and also for the White Wall. The lower level was vaulted and had three swivel-gun embrasures. There was at least one upper floor, provided with a latrine and gun embrasures. Sadly, the remainder of the west wall of the castle is now almost featureless.

First recorded in 1160, Berwick Castle once had nine towers around the walls and a magnificent array of buildings within. These included royal apartments, a great hall, chambers for the sheriff, a pantry, kitchen and buttery, a wardrobe tower, a forge, a bakery, larder and granary and a chapel. From the castle, a bridge led to a mighty barbican, or defensive forebuilding, called the Douglas or Percy Tower, which was set apart, between the town walls and the castle. After the construction of the Elizabethan walls, the castle became a disputed quarry, only relieved between 1604 and 1610 when the earl of Dunbar began to build a mansion within its walls. He never finished it, and it was abandoned on his death. The site subsequently returned to being quarried until the railway came – an inglorious end to one of the most important castles for both Scotland and England. Little now remains of the south, east or north curtain walls (except for Constable's Tower), or indeed the castle buildings. Little of the medieval town walls in this part of Berwick survive either.

Turn right onto the main road at the top of the footpath. Cross the bridge and then take the first road on the left, Northumberland Avenue.

The Castle to Lord's Mount

The main medieval gate, St Mary's Gate, once stood on Northumberland Avenue. The medieval wall then ran east, on the south side of this road. East of the modern houses, the wall can be seen once again. A considerable section of the original bank and ditch of Edward's defences and fragments of the stone wall, which quickly replaced the timber palisade, still survive.

Carry on down to the end of Northumberland Avenue

Beyond St Mary's Gate, the north wall was protected by at least three towers. No trace survives of the first two, but the bell tower remains. It was possibly built on the site of the 1336 Wallace Gate. In 1392 it was built, or possibly re-built as the Walls Tower for £28-13s-4d. It was again rebuilt and renamed in 1577 as a watchtower and bell tower to replace the bell in the corner tower. The bell was last rung in 1683.

Cross the grass to the other side of the bell tower and walk along the grass path until you reach Lord's Mount, on the left.

Lord's Mount

This massive curved stone bulwark was built in the 1540s to protect the walls at their weakest point. An earth bulwark had been built in front of the medieval bell tower in 1522, overlooking the long bank and ditch in the fields to the north of the walls, later recut and known as 'Spades Mire'. By 1539, however, the bulwark needed to 'be made smaller so that fewer men could guard...where the walls were weakest'. The construction of Lord's Mount marked a small but significant step in the development of military architecture. It has six vaulted gun casemates, each with expense magazines in the side walls, and smoke vents. The sills of the casemates originally had pin holes for swivel guns, which were later replaced by guns on simple carriages. There was once a kitchen here, and the remains of a fireplace can still be seen. The upper floor also has gun embrasures, but it was used principally for accommodation,

The bell tower

Above: Lord's Mount with the Bell Tower in the distance. Below: View looking west along Spades Mire

❖ GUNS ❖

Early vase-shaped guns appeared in Britain during the 1320s. They were of limited use, but their visible and audible impact was profound. They were initially made of copper or iron, but founders soon developed the skills to cast them in bronze. Guns were used more frequently as techniques improved, and by the end of the fourteenth century a rudimentary royal gunnery establishment served the English army during foreign campaigns. In 1380, the walls of the Tower of London had eleven guns and within five years Berwick had almost twice that number. These twenty guns might not have been the first seen at Berwick; it has been suggested that Edward III might have used guns here in 1333 after the Battle of Halidon Hill. If so, they would have been a novelty, with little practical value. The arming of the walls between 1384 and 1386, however, marked the

Cannon from the Crimea mounted on Fisher's Fort

beginning of the change from a castellated defence to an artillery fortification. Thereafter, each successive architectural change to the walls took account of attacking guns.

After 1386 Berwick was never without its protecting ordnance, and by 1533, there were 95 cannon bristling from the wall-heads of the castle and town, on top of all of the towers and gates. Within the towers were a further 191 small guns known as 'hagbuts'. These served a similar, anti-personnel role as the later muskets. One of the express aims of reducing the length of wall after 1538 was the need to reduce the number of expensive guns and gunners protecting the town. However, this seems not to have been achieved, since as late as 1689 it was suggested that the town required close to 90 guns to be secure. Despite several attempts to remove all of the guns, some stayed until 1918, when the last of the armament was finally removed from Windmill Bastion.

A cast bronze muzzle-loading Bastard Culverin, on a reproduction gun carriage, recovered from the Mary Rose. Similar guns would once have been used at Berwick

THE MARY ROSE TRUST, PORTSMOUTH

with an upper gun deck behind a parapet. In 1547, Lord's Mount was stocked with 15 cannon, plus eight hagbuts for hand use.

Leave Lord's Mount and take the lower path by the golf course.

Lord's Mount to Cowport

From the path, short sections of the walls are visible up to the ditch of Brass Bastion. From the point of Brass Bastion is a dam and a sluice gate for holding water in this section of the ditch.

Brass Bastion

Brass Bastion, built between 1563 and 1564, is the point where the old and new walls meet. The problem of how to breach the old walls, without leaving the town exposed, was only solved by a compromise that left the bastion far from symmetrical and its gorge so narrow that the back section of each of the flankers had to be arched over to provide an adequate path to the upper gun platforms. The flankers here were criticised while they were being built and they were widened at once. As elsewhere, the earth cavalier for the upper guns was added in 1639. The cobbled path over the rear arch of the west flanker is the only visible section of the original sentry path.

Traverse and Cowport

The path beside Brass Bastion follows the counterscarp of the ditch southwards, past the west end of the Traverse, known locally as 'the

Cowport, the last of the Elizabethan gates to survive largely intact

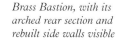

Brass Bastion, with its arched rear section and rebuilt side walls visible

The Traverse

Covered Way'. This was an earthwork built between 1564 and 1565 to close off the vulnerable Magdalene Fields to the east of the town.

Enter the Cowport, the last of the Elizabethan Gates still standing

Although it was planned as part of the Elizabethan Walls, it was only just completed in the queen's lifetime. Inside the gateway arch was once a portcullis, and the slots are still visible.

To complete the tour of the walls, turn right through Cowport and follow the path back onto the ramparts. Follow the path past Brass Bastion to Cumberland Bastion.

Cumberland Bastion

Cumberland Bastion, originally called Middle Mount, is one of the earliest and best preserved of the bastions. It is similar in appearance to Windmill Bastion. The flankers, particularly the east one, were remodelled in 1564. The door to the upper gun-deck and some of its joist holes survive at the rear of the flanker. (This can be seen from the ramparts; alternatively, the east flanker can be entered through the original tunnel entrance, just behind the rampart through the iron gate.) The remainder

View from Cumberland Bastion looking towards Brass Bastion. The cannon in the foreground is a cast-iron 6-pdr rose and crown dating from 1710

❖ THE GARRISON ❖

By the fifteenth century, the garrison at Berwick consisted of the governor, 500 men-at-arms, 8 captains, 80 horsemen and 70 gunners. A victualler attended to their daily needs: he agreed the price of lodgings and food, ensured that the mills worked and that the granaries and storehouses were stocked. The treasurer had the unenviable task of finding money to pay the garrison and the builders working on the fortifications, as well as paying their suppliers. As the numbers of guns increased, a master of ordnance became responsible for the safe storage of guns and powder and the regular maintenance of the guns.

A copy of the 'Ancient Statutes of the Town and Castle of Barwick [sic]', issued to the garrison in 1560 has survived. Loyalty to the queen was the first priority. There were to be no communications with Scots on pain of being taken as a traitor. A severe punishment awaited anyone passing on the daily password. Death was the only punishment for forging keys to the gates and selling the queen's guns. Loss of three days' pay was the punishment for soldiers not wearing their 'jacket of the queen's colours, white and green'. Similar penalties were issued for using 'any vile occupation or comonlie fishing for any white fish or salmon', or for using 'dice or

cards for money but at Christmas'. Access must be denied for anyone wishing to 'measure the length or depth or breadth thereof deceitfully'.

The rules forbade soldiers from accepting double pay, except on the fortifications, which suggests that some soldiers must have been 'moon-lighting' more lucratively elsewhere. Fighting and theft were forbidden but they remained frequent problems. With the rules, however, came responsibilities, and the regulations include a consider-able list of captains and gunners from the 'old establishment' who received pensions.

Engraving of the barrack square from Fuller's History of Berwick

Meg's Mount from the east

of the masonry was dismantled and splayed out to make it wider. This meant that the original cross walls had to be demolished and rebuilt. They were later repaired in 1747.

Meg's Mount

Continuing west from Cumberland Bastion, the wall continues over the top of Scotsgate. Originally resembling Cowgate, it was rebuilt and widened in 1815 and altered again in 1858. Work started in 1558 on the eastern half of Meg's Mount and the wall towards Cumberland Bastion. Meg's Mount was planned as a complete bastion, but the long-awaited wall from King's Mount never arrived. Meg's Mount, therefore, remains a demi-bastion.

Go through Scotsgate and down Marygate, and then left into Walkergate. This will take you back to the barracks. From the Parade, turn right down Ravensdowne.

The Hospital

150 metres along the road on the right-hand side (69a Ravensdowne) is a mid-eighteenth-century house, built in 1745 as a military hospital. In 1799, it contained 24 beds for the sick and a surgery, but it was considered too small for a complete regiment. It is now a private house.

Above: View of Scotsgate from the south

Right: The hospital

THE HISTORY OF
BERWICK-UPON-TWEED

❖

A Scottish Town

Berwick was already a large and prosperous Scottish burgh and port when David I of Scotland came to the throne in 1124. As well as being a centre of commerce, it had a royal castle, a mint and a considerable population. David I pushed the border south during his reign, ruling over most of Cumbria, Northumberland and far into North Yorkshire. England pressed to regain these lands, and the first major success came in 1174 with the capture of William the Lion at Alnwick. As a result, Berwick, Roxburgh and Edinburgh Castles were forfeited to the English crown.

Richard I of England sold back the Scottish gains to finance his crusades, but cross-border conflict continued. In 1216, when the English barons rebelled, many of the northern English lords declared their allegiance to Scotland. King John retaliated, and in Berwick 'with his own hand, contrary to the practice of kings, he disgracefully set fire to the house in which he had stayed'.

Berwick already had defences by August 1291, when Edward I of England came to the castle to hear the petitions over the disputed Scottish throne. Edward's choice, John Balliol, turned out to be a disappointment, so in 1296, after the Scots had confirmed their independence and ratified a treaty with France, Edward decided that direct rule was the only answer. The first action of Edward's 1296 campaign was the capture of Berwick as a military base for his

John Balliol offers homage to Edward I

The White Wall

conquest of Scotland. On 30 March 1296, the king crossed the Tweed with an army of 35,000 soldiers and besieged the town. Despite a stout defence, it was to no avail. The army 'attacked the gates, and passed through and won the town and by his gracious power killed 25,700 people'. The surrender of the castle and its garrison of 200 men followed later in the day. Although the accounts may exaggerate the numbers, they are united about the 'wretched slaughter' of the soldiers of the garrison and the citizens of Berwick. Indeed, those who survived were driven out of the town. Edward remained there for a month, ordering improvements to the defences on the north side of the town, with a 'high dyke of turf' and a deep ditch '80 feet wide and 40 feet deep' with 'great long stakes fixed on the top of it'.

He created a new administration for the conquest of Scotland and work began almost at once to secure Berwick as his stronghold. Operations stalled for a time when the king's treasurer, 'a pompous and proud man...did not build the stone wall which the king had ordered to be built'. Work proceeded between 1297 and 1298, with the construction of the bridge to the castle, the White Wall and a wall by the sea, beneath the Snook on the east of the town. In addition, the castle was repaired and supplies were delivered, including 'the coles burnt in the wine cellars to save the wines by reasons of the bitter cold'.

As work progressed in Berwick, Edward's campaigns in Scotland took two steps forwards and one step backwards, but throughout the campaigns, Berwick retained its role as a stronghold. In March 1306 the countess of Buchan crowned King Robert I in Scotland. He fled north and continued the fight against England. Meanwhile, the countess was captured by the English and forced to spend the next four years in a cage 'made in the likeness of a crown and suspended in the open air' from Berwick Castle, for her part in the coronation. The death of Edward I in 1307, and the significant victory at Bannockburn in June 1314 boosted Robert I's hold on power. But Berwick, along with the castles at Roxburgh and Lochmaben, stayed firmly in English hands, in spite of two failed attempts to storm the town. This was perhaps surprising, since the commander of the English garrison wrote to the king reminding him that of the 300 men-at-arms in Berwick he could not muster 50 because 'they are dying of hunger on the walls or deserting'.

The Scots retook Berwick in 1318, and set about repairing and heightening the defences. A new wall was built between the castle and the town, and the elaborate defences protecting the main gate into the castle were strengthened. Construction had started on a mighty gatehouse tower in 1303, but the Scots finished the task and named it after Robert I's closest friend, Sir James Douglas. (It was later renamed the Percy Tower, after another governor of Berwick, Henry, earl of Northumberland.) Work began on returning the castle to a pleasant residence. Robert I paid a merchant of Bruges for various colours 'brought for painting the King's chamber'.

Make Do and Mend

In the 1330s, when Edward Balliol failed in his attempt to take back the Scottish throne, Edward III took matters into his own hands. Retaking Berwick after a long siege, he began repair work again. The accounts of work done in Berwick in the fourteenth century provide us with a picture of the town. By 1344 a stone wall, with 19 towers and five gates, now replaced the turf dyke. The gates, walls and towers all had timber superstructures. Some of the gates were of a considerable size and they all required frequent repair. St Mary's Gate and Wallace's Gate housed prisons and by 1367 Wallace's Gate was provided with 'a barbican of a fort, with a base of stone and its upper part of earth' to protect the approach. Despite all of this work, a report in 1368 from the town authorities lamented the state of the fortifications. Raids by the Scots continued to damage the

The Siege of Berwick, 1296, from the fifteenth-century St Alban's Chronicle. This romantic depiction of Edward I's army besieging Berwick was drawn more than a century later to demonstrate the king's prowess and is not an accurate record of Berwick at the time

defences. In November 1355, a Scottish party scaled the walls and held the town until early the next year. Further repairs in 1367 proved insufficient to keep out the enemy, and in 1378, another raid resulted in the undermining of the castle walls. The town received its first delivery of artillery and gunpowder in 1384. More arrived in 1386 to fend off such attacks, when 'our artillery bought or received...for stocking of our said town, and also for the purchase of bells called Wachebelles, and cannon, and for the making of the said bells and cannons when they are broken'.

In 1405 the friends of Henry Percy, earl of Northumberland, thought Berwick strong enough to hold it rebelliously against their king, Henry IV. The retrieval operation that inevitably followed was swift, and it was very significant, as it was the first conflict in Britain certainly fought out using guns. Meanwhile, pressure from Scotland grew. Between 1459 and 1460, James II of Scotland laid siege to Roxburgh Castle and let it be known that Berwick would be next. Before he could act on the threat, however, he found an unwelcome place in history as the first monarch killed by gunpowder, when 'mair qurious than befits the majesty of a king' he stood too close to a cannon that exploded. Roxburgh and Berwick were retaken by the Scots in a treaty soon afterwards. This last, short period of Scottish rule in Berwick saw the usual repair

A street market in Marygate nestles beneath Berwick's imposing town hall

and rearming. Before he was finally forced to relinquish control of the town in 1482, James III admitted the 'grete charge and coist that his majestes has now taking apone him to hald and ly on heis aune expense the garaysoun of 500 men of war in the said toune for the keping of the defens thereof to the grete honour and profit of the Realme'.

Astonishingly, by 1500 neither country saw Berwick as either naturally or securely English, even though it had effectively been in English hands for 200 years. 'The English possess...in the kingdom of Scotland, the singular fortress of Berwick, after having belonged for a considerable time to each kingdom alternately... now King Henry the Seventh...has the command of all the eastern coast he can throw as many troops as he pleases.' (C. A. Sneyd (ed.), *A Relation of the Island of England about the Year 1500*, Camden Society, no. 37, 1847, p.17) There remained an implicit acknowledgement that Henry VII was going to need a considerable garrison to hold on to the town. The concern about Berwick did not diminish until James VI of Scotland was acknowledged as the heir to the English throne in the final years of the sixteenth century.

The Final Frontier

The construction of fortifications at Berwick relates directly to the political climate between England,

France and Scotland, with each lull in activity bringing a reduction in building works at Berwick. Between 1482 and 1524, in the wake of various crises, the walls and towers were lowered and backed with a considerable earth rampart called a 'countermure'. The tower roofs were lowered, strengthened and stocked with guns and, in 1491, a 'newe stone bulwerke' was built in the sands. 1509 saw a flurry of activity, rising to sheer panic in 1514, despite the resounding English victory at Flodden in the previous year.

Work began in earnest between 1522 and 1523, when the French forces, supporting Scotland and accompanying the duke of Albany, threatened the town. Richard Cavendish, a gunner, built an earthen bulwark to protect the vulnerable north-eastern corner. He also designed the D-shaped 'Great Bulwarke in the Snook' to protect the east flank of the town. Albany returned to France in 1524, and the citizens of Berwick breathed a sigh of relief. But deteriorating relations in 1530 brought the king's Master of Ordnance in person to Berwick and 300 men begin repairing the walls and replacing the White Wall postern. Work started within a year on Lord's Mount – a new and innovative fortification at the Bell Tower. Lord's Mount was of great interest to Henry VIII, and indeed, he might have had a hand in its

design. This massive semicircular artillery fortification provided a wide field of fire for the guns that bristled from at least two levels. It might have prolonged the life of the medieval walls but it was expensive. This approach to the town continued to give concern, and so to reinforce the defences beyond Lord's Mount, the long bank and ditch known as Stirling Dike was reconstructed. It is now known as Spades Mire but was first recorded in 1320 as the Bardyk, when it was already ancient.

In 1545, French forces returned to Scotland to support her against attempts to force the betrothal of Queen Mary to the young Edward VI. The earl of Hertford's army invaded Scotland in 1545 and 1547. This 'rough wooing' failed, but it saw Berwick stretched at the seams, with 20,000 men mustered here before the 1547 campaign.

By 1550 it was obvious that the cost of maintaining two miles of walls was prohibitive. Although many of the alterations made during

Interior of Lord's Mount showing one of the ground-floor gun casements and a fireplace

Bird's-eye view of Berwick Castle in 1689. Guns still top the walls and towers, although the interior buildings are reduced to domestic use

Henry VIII's reign were state-of-the-art, the defences were generally in a poor state of repair. Sir Richard Lee and Sir Thomas Palmer came to strengthen the town, and they proposed building an Italianate, rectangular fort with an angled-bastion at each of the corners, straddling the existing east wall. Work continued for six years and, although it was never completed, it was considered serviceable.

In 1557 the English Queen Mary lost Calais, so the French encouraged their Scottish allies to attack Berwick. As a result, Lee returned to Berwick with instructions to fortify the town. He proposed to build a ditch, earth ramparts and bastions around the town, within the old walls, abandoning the castle, the northern third of the town and the harbour. Costs escalated, and Lee faced constant criticisms. The flankers of the bastions were too narrow for manoeuvring guns, the structural supports for the ramparts were excessive and the exclusion of Magdalene Fields and the harbour were considered foolhardy. Because of the adverse comments, Lee stayed away from Berwick between 1561 and 1562. The governor appealed to Sir William Cecil to send him back with more funds, because there were no tools for the Irish labourers and the English masons abused the paymaster and finally mutinied. During Lee's frequent absences, his deputy engineer, Rowland Johnson, got on with the work. Building started in the north, and the first year saw the partial construction of Meg's Mount and Cumberland Bastion and the scarp of the north curtain wall. Before Brass Bastion was completed, however, the engineers had to decide how best to breach the old walls safely. In 1562 and 1563 a crisis in France depleted both the work-force and the funds. But the following year Lee returned and devised a method of minimising the risk by keeping the old walls standing as long as possible. He also had alterations made to the flankers, widening them from 21 to 34 feet and disposing of the upper gun-decks. A compromise was eventually reached over the security of the peninsula; it took the form of an additional earthwork, called the Traverse, crossing from just south of Brass Bastion to the sea.

Work limped on until 1569, a year after Mary Queen of Scots had fled Scotland and thrown herself at the mercy of Queen Elizabeth. The Elizabethan fortifications alone cost £128,648-5s-9^1/2d and a total of £250,000 had been spent in the sixteenth century.

In 1603, James VI and I ordered the garrison at Berwick to be reduced to 100 men, but peace was short-lived. Charles I's attempts to subdue the Scottish Church resulted in the Bishops' War of 1638 and Berwick was once again in the firing line. The earl of Essex occupied Berwick in April 1639. King Charles arrived a month later and peace with Scotland was signed here on 7 June. But the uneasy peace again turned to war.

Early in the English Civil War in 1643, Berwick successfully resisted the earl of Newcastle's attack and the Scottish army in England continued to hold the town until it was disbanded in 1645. During Oliver Cromwell's protectorate, Berwick remained a garrison frontier town, and became important once again. Improvements and repairs continued until 1653, by which time the earth parapet on the ramparts was raised and the bastions were completed by the raising of the cavaliers.

After the Civil War, the garrison was again reduced, but the soldiers of the new standing army took their billets, as they regularly marched to and from the trouble spots to the north. In 1705 the town authorities saw the possibility of relief in the prospect of town barracks, an entirely new concept.

A Design for Living

The Spanish word 'barraca' (meaning a hut) passed into English use in the late seventeenth century. Soldiers' lodgings existed long before. Indeed, there are examples as early as the 1540s of accommodation provided for the 'guards and garrisons' in forts and fortified castles on the Scottish Border, for example at Lauder and Roxburgh. Within 40 years other royal castles, including Tynemouth Castle, near Newcastle (also in the care of English Heritage), had lodgings. Tents provided the inspiration for

Portrait of Elizabeth I by Biagio Rebecca, after Marcus Gheeraerts the Younger, from Audley End

❖ A SOLDIER'S DAY ❖

'*As I have promised to tell the soldier's life in his barrack, suffice it briefly told. Some barracks are very comfortable, and others are not so.*'

(Thomas Jackson, 1814)

A soldier's day was strictly structured: 'Some reader may wish to know the daily routine of my duties', wrote a recruit in the Durham Light Infantry. 'I rose at five o'clock in the morning; and made up my bed; which occupied at least a quarter of an hour; and was a rather tiresome job. I made my toilet and at six turned out for drill, from which we were dismissed at quarter to eight when we breakfasted. From ten till twelve we were again at drill; had dinner at one in the shape of potatoes and meat, both usually of the most wretched quality; at two fell in for another drill, which terminated at four; after which hour my time was at my own disposal until tattoo, provided I was not ordered on picquet [guard duty].' The soldiers spent an extraordinary amount of time marching and drilling in time, but almost none training to fight or keeping fit. Uniforms and equipment were ill fitting and badly designed. Shoes were interchangeable and regularly swapped from right to left, to ensure even wear, with inevitable discomfort.

One of the smoke drawings found on the ceiling in the barracks during repair works in the 1980s. This one shows three men in tricorn hats; others show the Town Hall and soldiers' names

the structures, with small rooms for four or six men, built side by side and back to back and, eventually, on top of one another. The resulting blocks were two rooms deep and two storeys high, often large enough to accommodate several companies of soldiers.

Governments, however, do not invest in bricks and mortar for the comfort of soldiers alone. Barracks were built to contain soldiers, keeping them under supervision and out of view of a suspicious and sometimes hostile population. Before the mass recruitment wars in the present century, the army was considered to be a drain on taxes and more often a symbol of oppression.

The initial requests for barracks in Berwick were ignored, until the 1715 Jacobite Rising caught the Government unprepared. In Berwick, Captain Thomas Phillips, a Board of Ordnance engineer, put the walls into a state of readiness. Jacobite forces never seriously threatened the town, but Berwick's role as an important staging-post was recognised.

Early in 1716, the Board of Ordnance decided to build barracks. A year later, Captain Phillips received plans and estimates for the barracks and was asked to provide a report on the availability of materials. A site was chosen 'on the King's own Ground by the Town wall'. Materials were ordered: timber from Norway, over a million bricks from Tweedmouth, tile, lime, stone and slate locally and the doors and windows from the Tower of London. By June 1717, Mr Phillips only had to answer one or two outstanding questions, 'then directions will be given for proceeding with the foundations'.

By the end of 1718 the work was well underway, but, as ever, funds were scarce and the costs increased by a third. Andrew Jelfe altered the design for the entry at the point of building in 1719. The barracks were ready for fitting out in 1721, but the Board of Ordnance declared it had no funds to supply furniture and fittings. But John Sibbet, the newly appointed barrack master, seems to have found supplies.

The last repairs to the walls followed the 1745 Jacobite Rising. Few changes were made to the walls, but the gates were modified: Scotsgate was enlarged and Ness Gate was inserted in 1815, and ten years later Bridge Gate was removed.

In 1856, the Government proposed to sell the barracks, but the town objected because 'it will be a great blow to the prosperity and spirit of the town'. The French invasion alarms of 1858 saved the barracks

❖ FAMILY LIFE ❖

Soldiers needed permission from the army to marry, and their wives faced the prospect of years without a home, only able to earn half rations by washing the officers' linen. Before the advent of married quarters, a blanket hung across the corner of the barrack room was often the only privacy a wife could expect. Children slept where they could, on the benches or under the beds. Foreign service for a regiment left many families to fend for themselves at home. For those allowed to travel with their husbands, life was precarious. They spent years under canvas, often rather too close to battlefields for comfort, and always facing the prospect of abandonment or a rushed second marriage should their husbands die.

The inscription beneath this engraving reads:

A luckless day last Whitsuntide!
When my faithful Soldier died.
His tent which stands near yonder tree
Affords no shelter now for me.

The Soldier's Wife, *published by E Walker, 1793*

and led to the construction of a coastal defence battery on Windmill Bastion, manned by the Berwick Artillery Volunteers after 1861. Houses were built against the walls, and it was not until 1903 that the importance of the walls was recognised. As a result the Office of Works (later English Heritage) took some of the remains into care, with more following in 1931. The Berwick Historic Monuments Committee, set up locally, promoted the conservation of the walls. Their work was both practical and effective. Despite their efforts, buildings continue to be constructed up to the fortifications. It was not until the King's Own Scottish Borderers marched out for the last time in 1964 that Berwick finally lost its military role.

Dr Fuller's drawing of soldiers on parade in front of the barracks, from his History of Berwick *(1799)*

Further Reading

James Douet, *British Barracks 1600–1914: Their Architecture and Role in Society*, London, 1998

Richard Hewlings, 'Hawksmoor's Brave Designs for the Police', in *English Architecture Public and Private*, John Bold and Edward Chaney (eds.), London and Rio Grande, 1993, pp.215–29

Iain MacIvor, 'The Elizabethan Fortifications of Berwick-upon-Tweed', *Antiquaries Journal*, Vol. xlv (1965), pp.67–70

Iain MacIvor, 'Places of Strength in the Lothians and the East Border, 1513–42' in *Scottish Weapons and Fortifications 1100–1800*, David Caldwell (ed.), Edinburgh, 1981, pp.94–152

The History of the Kings Works, H. M. Colvin (ed.), Vol. II (1963), pp.563–71; Vol. IV (1982), pp.613–44